Science Fiction Films

edited by
Thomas R. Atkins

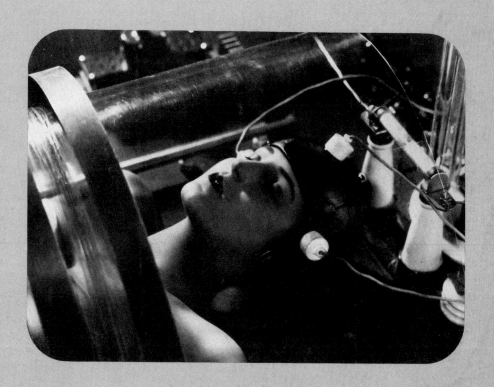

MONARCH PRESS

791.43
Science...

Standard Book Number: 671-08100-4

Library of Congress Catalog Card Number: 75-23543

Designed by Denise Biller

Published by
MONARCH PRESS
a division of Simon & Schuster, Inc.
1 West 39th Street
New York, N.Y. 10018

CONTENTS

Many nights Fiorello Bodoni would awaken to hear the rockets sighing in the dark sky. He would tiptoe from bed, certain that his kind wife was dreaming, to let himself out into the night air. For a few moments he would be free of the smells of old food in the small house by the river. For a silent moment he would let his heart soar alone into space, following the rockets.

Ray Bradbury
"The Rocket"

All that night we sped beneath the hurtling moons of Mars, as strange a company as was ever foregathered upon any planet, I will swear. Two men, each possessing the body of the other, an old and wicked empress whose fair body belonged to a youthful damsel beloved by another of this company, a great white ape dominated by half the brain of a human being, and I, a creature of a distant planet, with Gor Hajus, the Assassin of Toonol, completed the mad roster.

Edgar Rice Burroughs
"The Master Mind of Mars"

CONTRIBUTORS

THOMAS R. ATKINS is Chairman of the Theatre Arts Department at Hollins College, Va., and Editor-Publisher of *The Film Journal.* He has done books for Simon & Schuster, Indiana University Press, and Doubleday.

LEE ATWELL studied film at USC and UCLA and worked for two years on the American Film Institute catalogue. He has published criticism in *Film Quarterly* and other magazines.

FRED CHAPPELL is Writer-in-Residence at the University of North Carolina at Greensboro. He has written a book of poetry, *The World Between the Eyes,* and four novels, the most recent entitled *The Gaudy Place.*

VIVIAN SOBCHACK teaches film at the University of Utah and has published articles in *The Journal of Popular Film* and *Film/Literature Quarterly.*

GENE D. PHILLIPS teaches fiction and film at Loyola University of Chicago. He is the author of *The Movie Makers: Artists in an Industry* and *Graham Greene: The Films of His Fiction.*

STUART M. KAMINSKY teaches in the Division of Radio-TV-Film at Northwestern University. His work has appeared in many periodicals, and he has recently published books on Don Siegel and Clint Eastwood.

ACKNOWLEDGMENTS

The essays by Fred Chappell, Vivian Sobchack, and Lee Atwell appeared originally in *The Film Journal*, Vol. II, No. 3. Gene D. Phillips' interview with Lang is an excerpt from a longer conversation printed in *Focus on Film*, Vol. V. Stuart Kaminsky's essay and interview with Don Siegel are from *Cinefantastique*, Vol. II, No. 3.

The editor wishes to thank John Baxter, the Memory Shop, Cinemabilia, as well as the Film Stills Archives of the Museum of Modern Art and the British Film Institute, for providing many of the illustrations and photographs in this book.

The editor is also grateful to Hollins College for the Mellon grant and leave of absence to work on this book and others in the Monarch film series.

PREFACE

The essays in this book offer a comprehensive re-evaluation of science fiction on the screen from George Méliès' *A Trip to the Moon* and Fritz Lang's *Metropolis* to contemporary films like Stanley Kubrick's *2001: A Space Odyssey* and Andrei Tarkovski's *Solaris*. The illustrations, many of them rare and unique, have been selected to provide a visual survey of some of the genre's most memorable images.

Fred Chappell's essay explores the rich multiplicity of images and the characteristic motifs linking films as diverse as *King Kong*, *The Incredible Shrinking Man*, and *Alphaville*. Vivian Sobchack focuses on low budget but imaginative fifties films like *The Thing*, *Them!*, and *It Came from Outer Space*, in which Jack Arnold and other directors used familiar terrain to create unsettling visions of man's precarious existence on earth.

Invasion of the Body Snatchers, Don Siegel's masterpiece of psychological horror set in a small California town, is analyzed by Stuart Kaminsky and also discussed by the director. Finally, Lee Atwell examines a Soviet filmmaker's haunting parable of cosmonauts exploring an enigmatic sea on an alien planet. Adapted from a novel by the Polish writer Stanislas Lem, *Solaris* is widely regarded as one of the most impressive of recent science fiction films.

NOTES ON
SCIENCE FICTION
ON THE SCREEN

Thomas R. Atkins

In the early fifties when Howard Hawks' *The Thing from Another World* came to Mobile, Alabama, I was twelve and, like most of my companions, a compulsive moviegoer hooked on the weekend matinee ritual. Every Saturday at our neighborhood theatres, the Azalea, the Roxy, or the Loop, we sat in the darkness, anonymous rows of bodies glutting ourselves on candy, Cokes, and B-movies. In those afternoon double and triple features, the Hollywood studios fed us a steady diet of familiar formulas — gangster pictures, horror shows, westerns, comedies, serials, and cartoons — the majority of them as cheap, predictable, and instantly gratifying as the salted popcorn we consumed. The science fiction formula appeared less frequently on our screens, except in space opera serials, until the popularity of George Pal's *Destination Moon* and Hawks' *The Thing* stimulated a revival of the genre.

The lobby posters and coming attractions trailers for *The Thing* convinced us that the alien would be more hideous and its story more awesome than anything we had yet encountered in our matinee fantasies. When it finally arrived at the Azalea, the smallest and rowdiest theatre, we found that the movie lived up to its publicity, despite the fact that the Thing itself — a humanoid carrot that

The Thing from Another World

thrived on blood — remained offscreen most of the time. From the opening flaming credits to the reporter's final warning, "Tell the world . . . watch the skies," the usually raucous audience was either stunned into silence or shrieking in terror. After leaving the theatre, we immediately abandoned our routine games of cops and robbers or cowboys and Indians and began enacting another drama: soldiers and scientists combating a hostile invasion. We fought over who would play the creature and forced smaller kids to do sound effects — the howling of the huskies, the dripping of the ice block, the noise of the geiger counter, and the moaning of the Polar wind.

At the time we had no idea that *The Thing* was the beginning of a cycle of films that would continue to enliven our games and haunt our dreams for years. Throughout most of the Eisenhower decade, with its constant news of UFO sightings, Red spies, air raid

The Beast from 20,000 Fathoms

Forbidden Planet

drills, and bomb shelters, we escaped to our movie houses to watch *War of the Worlds, It Came from Outer Space, Them!, Creature from the Black Lagoon, Godzilla, This Island Earth,* and *I Married a Monster from Outer Space,* to name only a few titles of the numerous sf films of the fifties. None of us could have guessed or would have even cared that some of these films happened to be durable works of art retaining their power to disturb and fascinate audiences today.

ACADEME DISCOVERS SF

Once totally dismissed by most scholars and viewed with suspicion by critics, the science fiction film genre is currently enjoying a new respect and recognition as a serious form of cinematic art.

Catalogues from colleges across the country list courses dealing with various aspects of the sf film; students now study *Forbidden Planet* and *The Monolith Monsters* with an earnestness traditionally reserved for *Birth of a Nation* and *Citizen Kane*.

In 1974, moreover, the American Film Institute co-sponsored with the World Science Fiction Convention a retrospective of fourteen films at the Kennedy Center in Washington, D.C. (two of the

© *1975 by William M. Gaines*

films shown, *The Day the Earth Stood Still* and *Earth Versus the Flying Saucers,* are set in the capital city); and the Hayden Planetarium in New York City offered a special summer course, "The Universe of Science Fiction Film," featuring presentations and discussions of ten films.

Yet, despite the aura of academic respectability now associated with the genre, it is important to remember that the science fiction film, like other studio formulas, is not closely related to literature, poetry, or to any type of art aimed at a limited audience but is essentially a form of popular entertainment with roots in the Saturday matinee experience. Because its potential is chiefly visual and emotional rather than intellectual, the sf film usually communicates to the instinctive child in us instead of the reflective adult. Like all movie genres, science fiction on the screen resists rigid academic classification or aesthetic definition; it is flexible and various, changing its outline and content to suit the needs and expectations of its audience. As John Baxter has observed in his *Science Fiction in the Cinema*, "Sf cinema is basically a sensuous medium. . . . Like the *bande-dessinée* (comic strip), sf film offers simple plots and one-dimensional characters in settings so familiar as to have the quality of ritual. It relies on a set of visual conventions and a symbolic language, bypassing intellect to make a direct appeal to the senses."

MÉLIÈS THE MAGICIAN

The science fiction film genre was invented by a cartoonist and conjurer, Georges Méliès, who delighted audiences with magical spectacles at the Théâtre Houdin in Paris and turned to filmmaking in 1895 after attending a showing of the first moving pictures made by Louis and Auguste Lumière. The brief pictures shot by the Lumière brothers with their newly-invented cinématographe were primarily "actualités" or documentaries of real places and events — trains, boats, bicycles, parades, landmarks, animals, aquariums, babies, people at work and play. But Méliès eventually set up his camera inside a studio and created "artificially arranged scenes" either based on fictional stories or historical events transformed into fantastic tales. For such films as *Bluebeard*, *The Haunted Castle*, *The Dreyfus Case*, *The Eruption of Mont-Pelé*, *The Seven Deadly Sins*, and *Faust and Marguerite*, he not only designed the sets, costumes, and makeup but developed nearly all of the photographic tricks and special effects used today in sf films.

Borrowing ideas from the novels of Jules Verne and H. G. Wells, Méliès made his most famous and influential film, *A Trip to the Moon* (*Le Voyage dans la Lune*), which contains many of the basic ingredients of the sf genre: egotistical scientists, space travel, alien craters and grottos, bizarre plantlife, lobster-clawed monsters, and even attractive females. Méliès' attitude toward this unusual material is childlike and playful — as when the astronomers' space bullet lands in the eye of the man on the moon or when the Selenites vanish in explosions of smoke upon being struck by an umbrella. The tone of the film, as critic Harry Geduld has noted, is a remarkable mixture of satire and wonder. The first science fiction film is a mad voyage devised by a caricaturist with a surreal

*Méliès' original sketch for **A Trip to the Moon***

A Trip to the Moon

sense of humor and executed by a magician with a sure knowledge of how to astonish his audience. Not content merely to be director and designer, Méliès also gives a grandly comic performance as the leading earthman.

When *A Trip to the Moon* was released in 1902, its length and inventiveness did more than any previous film to convince other filmmakers and the public that the new motion picture medium had great creative potential. The entire sf genre, ranging from *Metropolis* and *Just Imagine* through the fifties monster cycle to contemporary films as different as *Barbarella*, *Planet of the Apes*, and *Zardoz*, derives in part from Méliès' experiments in his glass-ceilinged studio in a Paris suburb. More than half a century later, working in the elaborate sound stages of Pinewood Studios outside London, Stanley Kubrick created another landmark film, *2001: A Space Odyssey*, which continued the voyage begun in *A Trip to the Moon* and prompted a revival of popular as well as critical interest in the sf genre. Both films are basically conjurer's shows, appealing predominantly to the senses and offering what Méliès called "magical and mystical views" full of humor and awe.

One Million Years B.C.

Planet of the Apes

Conquest of the Planet of the Apes

Seconds

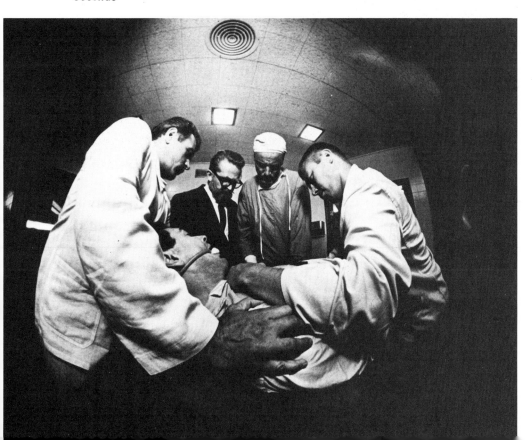

THX 1138

Zardoz

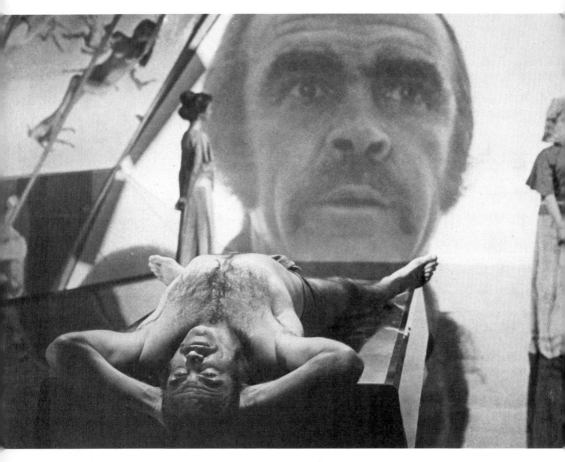

Zardoz

Fantastic Planet

2001: A Space Odyssey

FRITZ LANG ON METROPOLIS

Gene D. Phillips

Among the most impressive and imaginative of early science fiction films is Fritz Lang's *Metropolis*, a multi-million dollar production made in 1925-26 at UFA Studios in Berlin and described by the director as "a horror tale of the future." Set in the year 2000, his film concerns the revolt of a subterranean slave race against their oppressive masters who live in luxurious skyscrapers. Like Méliès, Lang also worked as a cartoonist; his film work reflects a brilliant sense of design. The evocative images of *Metropolis*, photographed by famed cinematographer Karl Freund, are the precursors of later film visualizations of nightmarish future societies such as *1984*, *Alphaville*, *Fahrenheit 451*, *THX 1138*, *La Jetée*, *Westworld*, and *Fantastic Planet*.

The following discussion of *Metropolis* is an excerpt from a longer interview that Gene D. Phillips conducted with Lang at his home in Beverly Hills, California.

PHILLIPS: Your trip to the United States for the premiere of *Die Nibelungen* in 1924 gave you the inspiration for *Metropolis*.

19 /

LANG: Erich Pommer, the chief executive at UFA Studios in Berlin, and I came over for the premiere, and for some reason we were considered enemy aliens and couldn't land in New York on the day that the boat docked. Instead we had to wait until the following day to disembark. That evening I looked from the ship down one of the main streets of New York and saw for the first time the flashing neon lights lighting up the street as if it were daytime. This was all new to me. I said to myself, what will a big city like this, with its tall skyscrapers, be like in the future? That started me thinking about *Metropolis*.

PHILLIPS: *Metropolis* enhanced your reputation as a director both in Germany and abroad, did it not?

LANG: But after I finished the film I personally didn't much care for it, though I loved it while I was making it. When I looked at it after it was completed I said to myself, you can't change the social climate of a country with a message like "The heart must be the go-between of the head (capital) and the hands (labor)." I was convinced that you cannot solve social problems by such a message. Many years later, in the 1950s, an industrialist wrote in *The Washington Post* that he had seen the film and that he very much agreed with that statement about the heart as go-between. But that didn't change my mind about the film.

PHILLIPS: Yet young people today, I have found, take the film very seriously.

LANG: In the later years of my life I have made a point of speaking with a lot of young people in order to try to understand their point of view. They all hate the establishment, and when I asked them what they disliked so intensely about our computerized society they said, "It has no heart." So now I wonder if Mrs. von Harbou, my scriptwriter on the film, was not right all the time when she wrote that line of dialogue for *Metropolis* a half century ago. Personally I still think that the idea is too idealistic. How can a man who has everything really understand a man who has very little?

PHILLIPS: Stanley Kubrick paid tribute to *Metropolis* in naming his 1968 film *2001* because your film takes place in the year 2000.

LANG: That never occurred to me, especially since I don't recall that any specific year is ever mentioned in *Metropolis*. In any event another thing that I didn't like about the picture afterwards were scenes like the one in which a worker is pictured having constantly to move the hands of the giant dial. I thought that that was too stupid and simplistic an image for man working in a dehumanizing, mechanized society. And yet years later when I was watching the astronauts on television I saw them lying down in their cockpit constantly working dials just like the worker in my film. It makes you wonder.

Lang sitting below camera, Freund behind camera during filming of **Metropolis**

Filming of **Metropolis,** Lang at far right

Metropolis set at UFA Studios

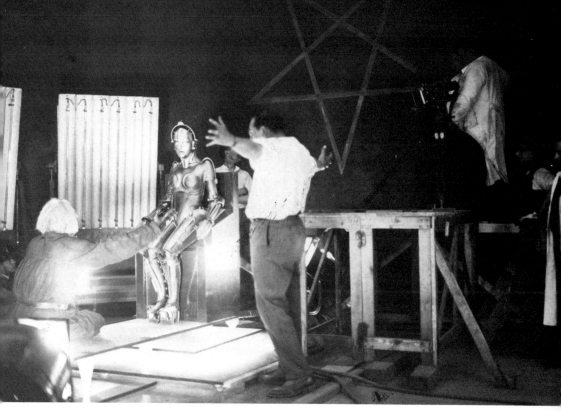

Lang directing a scene from **Metropolis**

Brigitte Helm as Maria

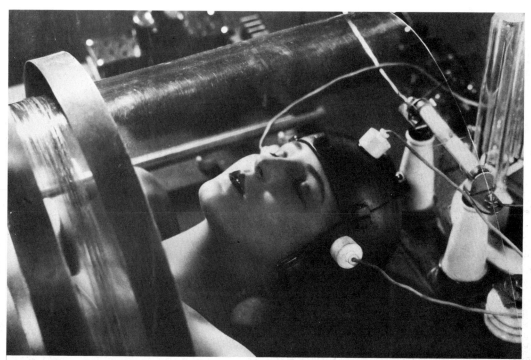

Rotwang's
female robot

Lang rehearsing the false Maria

The false Maria's seductive nightclub dance

Lang directing a scene in the underground city

Cameraman Freund during filming of **Metropolis**

Worker turning hands of giant dial in **Metropolis**

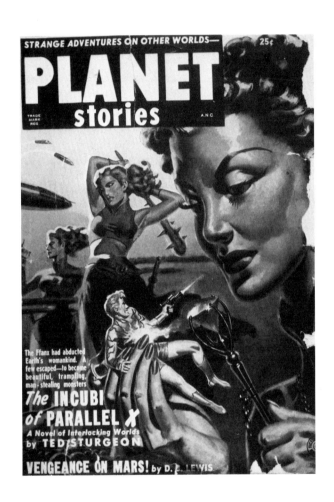

STRANGE ADVENTURES ON OTHER WORLDS—

25¢

PLANET
stories

TRADE
MARK
REG.

A.N.C

The Ffanx had abducted
Earth's womankind. A
few escaped—to become
beautiful, trampling,
man-stealing monsters

The INCUBI
of PARALLEL X
A Novel of Interlocking Worlds
by TED STURGEON

VENGEANCE ON MARS! by D. E. LEWIS

THE SCIENCE FICTION FILM IMAGE:
A TRIP TO THE MOON TO 2001: A SPACE ODYSSEY

Fred Chappell

Literary science fiction and film science fiction became two different kinds of expression about 1938. Before this date the two forms did not differ significantly in content or intention. After all, both the literature and the film were born together; Wells, Verne, and Méliès were contemporaries. And although we can draw valid contrasts between the emphases of Wells and Verne (the one speculative, the other extrapolative; Wells philosophic, Verne scientific), we do see a true common ground between them when we think of Méliès' films, in which ideas about the as yet undiscovered universe take visual shape. (For example, Méliès' *A Trip to the Moon* borrows images from the moon novels of both pioneer writers: Verne's propulsion, Wells' aliens.)

But in 1938 John W. Campbell became editor of *Astounding Science Fiction* (under his leadership to prove the most influential force in sf for twenty-five years) and he uttered an edict to the effect that fiction for his magazine should be written as if it were an adventure story for a magazine of the 23rd century. It would be hard not to sympathize with Campbell's ambitions. He aimed to get rid of the rather self-righteous ornamentation which often obscured the narrative line of earlier sf: all those long visual descriptions of futuristic settings, those deadly earnest scientific justifications, the bombastic exhortations to the reader to suspend disbelief. *Astounding* was, after all, a pulp magazine striving to survive in a restricted market with competition as tough as Dashiell Hammett, Raymond Chandler, *The Shadow*, Luke Short, *Ranch Romances*. In order to compete, the sf story had to accept more information as premise, as dossier; the story had to take place *on top of* the background information in order to acquire flexibility and point. The sf writer found himself in a position analogous to the jazz musician who was bored with playing the melodic line of some weary blues song, but who was still interested in treating the chord changes. The writer was simply asking his audience to take more for granted.

For Campbell's purposes the approach worked out just dandy. His writers were enabled to produce a more sophisticated, more streamlined (though not more literate) kind of story. But these gains were short term. Two corollaries of his dictum came nigh to vitiating the whole genre of sf. The first of these corollaries was that the premises of most sf stories would be pretty nearly identical. The fact that they were premises made them conventions, and surely no form of literature was ever saddled with so many narrative conventions: faster-than-light space travel, a densely populated universe, a pre-Victorian notion of civilized progress, benevolent or malevolent totalitarianism, protagonist as warrior-scientist, and so forth. The amount of ingenuity necessary to overcome these narrative handicaps was staggering. And — as every sophomore knows or else should know — mere ingenuity is one of the enemies of honest literature.

The second corollary was that there was very little in post-Campbell sf to look at. Conceptual conventions necessarily dictate visual images to a great extent. In reading a detective story of the twentieth century we do not expect to find detailed, explanatory descriptions of elevators or golf courses. Just so, reading a 23rd-century adventure story in *Astounding*, we do not expect to get longwinded descriptions of teleportation machines or spaceships or G-ray zygomatizers. These contraptions are merely the furniture amidst which the drama of the writer's ingenuity is enacted.

Again, ingenuity. Another unfortunate thing about a literature of ingenuity is that it does not properly belong to the act of writing at all, but rather to conversation. The ingenuity which comes up with a new wrinkle in a vicar's-rose-garden murder or a new time-travel paradox is produced by a desire to top what has been done before. It's the same impulse that causes us to say ever more outrageous things at cocktail parties, to find a more allusive stichomythic rejoinder, to get meaner and dirtier when we're playing "dozens." Fascinating in its own terms, and addictive; but about as visually interesting as peanut butter.

Early sf, whatever its faults, always gave the reader something to look at. Verne's enormous cannon is one of the least viable ways ever thought of to get men to the moon, but it is a grand image. (Méliès, realizing this fact, sexily ornamented the object in an almost Lubitsch-like manner with girls in brief costumes.) Wells' Selenites are ridiculous as life-forms for the moon, but they are entrancing to look at. (To which image Méliès added the allusion of the bluestockings of 18th-century salons.)

The images of early sf film were derived from the literature, but in the later fiction there were few images to use. The most fascinating image in ordinary sf is the imagined landscape (or, more often, cityscape) of the future or of an alien civilization. In the early films, in Méliès particularly, and afterward most famously in Lang's *Metropolis* (1926), in David Butler's *Just Imagine* (1930), and in William Cameron Menzies' *Things to Come* (1936) — and to some extent in the first Flash Gordon serial — we have these pure Utopian archetypal images. The crowded straight-lined megacities with their enticing anthropomorphic inventions, light and shadow berserkly romantic, and the feverishly clinical aura. . . . But after *Things to Come* this kind of image disappeared from film for thirty years, until *This Island Earth* and *Forbidden Planet* (1955) and, more importantly, *2001* (1968).

The megacity of the future remained the basic image for the fiction, but it was pushed to the background, and rarely was thoroughly enough realized to impinge upon the reader's senses. It became necessary for sf film to develop a basic image independent of the fiction, and this it did; film developed, in fact, a mul-

Just Imagine

Things to Come

tiplicity of basic sf images, almost all of them — predictably — derived from secondary themes or subdivisions of the genre. And all of them were contained in earlier films. The only difference was an identifying emphasis which marked such-and-such a film as belonging to the field of science fiction.

So, a multiplicity of basic images. Yet there was a single quality characteristic of all of them, the quality of incongruence. This was the same special, deliberate kind of incongruity we see in surrealist paintings. It is the kind of incongruity which makes

33 /

one stare and stare because of the confusion of emotional associations attached to different objects placed in the same visual frame.

The different kinds of incongruity which produce an identifiable sf film image can, I believe, be numbered at five. These incongruities are:

1. *Anachronisms: displacement of objects from their normal temporal contexts;*
2. *Scale: giantism or pygmyism;*
3. *Displacement of faculties or sympathies (e.g., intelligent machines, benevolent monsters, malevolent doctors, etc.);*
4. *Violent collision of natural and artificial objects (e.g., the spaceship in the wilderness, spacemen among alien aborigines, etc.);*
5. *Inaccuracy of detail: factual error displayed out of ignorance or out of concern for visual effect.*

The Day the Earth Stood Still

Of these five kinds of incongruity, scale is probably the most common numerically because of the fashion in the 1950s for giant menaces. But I believe that the first sort, anachronism of objects, is more nearly indispensable to the sf film image. And I will take as touchstone example the huge flying saucer of "liquid metal" which sits silent and ominous on the White House lawn in Robert Wise's *The Day the Earth Stood Still*. In a Méliès film, in *Things to Come* or *Metropolis*, a spacecraft, even a flying saucer, would not be incongruous because the viewer could take for granted that the technology needed to manufacture such a machine did exist, and also that the culture which produced it would have use for it. Its visual meaning in the Wise film is that the future has come to visit us, the flying saucer is an anomaly in time. This anomalous quality is aggravated when the saucer opens to disgorge the great robot Gort and Michael Rennie, ambassador of galactic peace, clad in a gold lamé rock and roll outfit.

Incongruence of temporal anomaly covers a great number of sf film images. It includes, of course, the images of all time travel films, and those in which Earth is visited by beings from other planets. It includes also all those films which center upon a marvelous invention, a machine "ahead of its time"; so that even serials like *The Mysterious Dr. Satan* in which the villains send out funny-looking robots to kill the heroes qualify. (This category includes one very famous non-image, Claude Rains as the Invisible Man.) The invention need not be destructive or even visually prepossessing in order to qualify. A mutant bacterium or unseen gas will do, and so will Alec Guinness's quite ordinary-looking clothing in *The Man in the White Suit*.

There is some obvious confusion between my first and fourth categories. A large amount of overlapping occurs because when the sf story is set in the present the normal visual environment is identified as the natural and the anomalous object as the artificial. In our touchstone image the White House lawn is Nature and the flying saucer is Artifice. But the fourth category does need to be maintained separately for other reasons.

Scale, our second category of incongruence, is too obvious to require much discussion. The attack of the giant shrimp or

King Kong

King Kong

amoeba or spermatozoon is as familiar a part of the cultural milieu of the 1950s as Elvis Presley or Big Daddy Lipscomb. I would propose two touchstone images: King Kong atop the Empire State Building and Grant Williams in his dollhouse in Jack Arnold's *The Incredible Shrinking Man*. The first image is chosen as a reminder that *King Kong* is, after all, a sf movie and belongs to the oldest subdivision of the genre, the extraordinary voyage. The second image is chosen because it belongs to a fine, and frequently overlooked, film — almost the only film which deals seriously with the theme of pygmyism. A rather brief film, *The Incredible Shrinking Man* is divided into four parts. The first part explains how Williams comes to be afflicted (overexposure to radiation and insecticides);

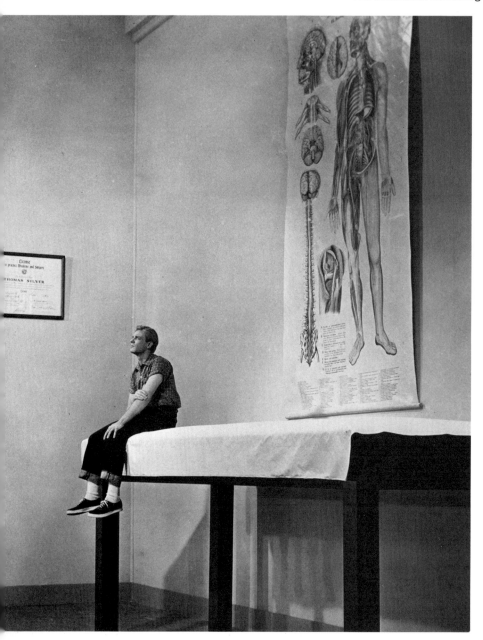

The Incredible Shrinking Man

next we are shown the social and sexual embarrassments of small people (he makes friends with a beautiful dwarf lady but continues to shrink); the third part develops the Robinson Crusoe aspect of the situation, dealing with how the man survives in the hostile environment of his basement after it is supposed that he was eaten by his cat (an exciting battle with a spider); the final part of the film attempts to consider some of the metaphysical implications. Williams has at last grown so small that he exits his house through the mesh of a window screen. He stands looking up at the stars, now so immeasurably far away, and intones in a sort of existential desperation: "*I still exist.*"

It ought to be noted too that disparity of scale is not always anomalous in intent. Our "norm" image for sf, the megacity, is gigantic in scale, but not anomalous. The immense stretches of time and space in Kubrick's *2001* are not factually anomalous, but they have for us the force of anomaly because our ordinary experience does not expose us to these facts. (And Godard's *Alphaville* neatly makes a point about scale: that bigness does not signify goodness. Here Akim Tamiroff plays probably the only Bowery derelict seen in a film about the future.)

The third category of incongruence, the displacement of (usually human) faculties and sympathies to other objects or roles, includes the most famous cliché in the whole of sf, the mad scientist or mad doctor. It makes no difference that daily experience and common sense may teach us quite otherwise, our expectations are that doctor/scientists are rational and well-disposed toward mankind. Sf stories quite early on began to frustrate or reverse our preconceptions both for shock value and in order to predicate an unnatural state of the universe — malevolent rather than benevolent or dispassionate. As touchstone image I would choose Rudolph Klein-Rogge as Rotwang in *Metropolis* rather than the more familiar Colin Clive as Frankenstein. Dr. Frankenstein is accidentally an agent of destruction, driven to extremes by overzealous devotion to his fixed idea, while Rotwang is evil by choice.

Metropolis

Rotwang's invention, the False Maria, is also an example of incongruous displacement, of faculty rather than sympathy. All images of robots represent this displacement, machines assuming the human faculty of intelligence. (It need not always be a human intelligence. The cutest robot of them all, the ubiquitous Robbie, who first appeared in *Forbidden Planet*, is considerably more akin to Lassie than to his creators.) Nor is high intelligence always conferred upon machines; it may be given to children, as in *The Damned* and *Village of the Damned*, to animals, as in *Island of Lost Souls*, and even to vegetables, as in *The Thing* and *Invasion of the Body Snatchers*.

41 /

Island of Lost Souls

Here too ought to be mentioned the Caliban motif, the visually repulsive monster who has the attribute of innocence or of moral injury. This phenomenon most commonly occurs in the Gothic horror films where it is usually a matter of faulty will-transference; Frankenstein's monster is really no more than Cesare the Somnambulist out of the control of his master. But sometimes sf borrows the ploy, as in *The Colossus of New York*.

As the extraordinary voyage was the oldest subdivision of sf literature, so did it remain the most common. Most magazine and book narratives concerned themselves with space travel and the exploration of other worlds, and for this reason the fourth category of film images, violent collision of the natural and the artificial, was the dominant image in the literature. This is the kind of incongruity you see on your television set when Eugene Cernan and Harrison Schmitt are galumphing about the moon, dressed in gleaming, hypersophisticated life-support systems, and sleeping by night in a contraption which looks like a potbellied coal stove gone stark crazy. These sights have been available to us for years, perhaps most notably in Lang's *Woman in the Moon* and George Pal's *Destination Moon*. The visitation of a complex scientific object which represents a highly technological society upon a lonely, trackless wilderness gives us an oxymoron of association. One cannot help wondering if the image would be less jarring if we could travel to the moon in birchbark canoes. The sensation is identical when a complex alien technology visits one of the un-trammeled areas of Earth, as in *It Came From Outer Space*. What is at stake here is a clash of current cultural values, and I should like to know my reaction at seeing a slim silver spaceship from planet Zamm IX come down in one of our huge municipal garbage dumps.

Village of the Damned

*Destination
Moon*

Douglas Trumball's *Silent Running* offers an interesting reversal of this visual colliding. This film gives us a forest with flowers, streams, and animals — the Edenic associations are deliberate — all contained in an enormous spaceship designed to preserve at least a part of our "natural environment," the world by this time having been totally trashed.

Our final category of incongruence is inaccuracy of detail, a matter which used to drive devotees of the literature to contemplate murder furiously. *Conquest of Space* and *When Worlds Collide* provide nearly inexhaustible funds of scientific solecisms which occur in almost all space movies. You know them already, the meteor which, flaming in airless space, goes whooshing by the spaceship with a loud and sinister sibilance, the orange rocket exhaust where there is no oxygen to burn, the spaceship that lands on its belly, and so on. These scientific errors constitute interesting incongruities, whether they existed in the films because of directorial ignorance, or whether they were entered deliberately in the interest of visual excitement. The latter reason must have obtained often, for many of the errors in film are reiterations of the errors of the cover illustrations of the pulp magazines. (To which illustrations the later films owe a great deal.)

Error persisted so long and so blatantly that it became a sf film tradition, and another way in which *2001* has acquired the surprise of anomaly without actually being anomalous is in its insistent accuracy. We are so used to traditional error that the truth shocks us. Kubrick had the imagination to derive surprise and beauty from the facts of the case. When his ship Aries lands on the moon there is no big burst of red flame but instead a great white cloud of lunar dust. (I know people who applauded that sequence in the theaters because they admired Kubrick's powers of observation.) Seen from space, the ship moves along slowly and daintily (the waltz tune underscoring the movement); but when the vehicle is seen with the lunarscape in the foreground we note that it is actually traveling at a tremendous rate of speed. Without pushing the notion too hard, one might suggest that William Carlos Williams' idea, the poetry of fact, "no ideas but in things," is utilized in these frames.

There is one other image, common to many sf films, so common that it almost deserves a separate category. This image is the double, encountered in such films as *4-Sided Triangle* and *Voyage to the Far Side of the Sun*. But the image of the double is prevalent in many kinds of films — romances (twin sisters), detective stories (the long-lost identical twin), horror films — and the only way the sf double is distinguishable is by a pseudoscientific explanation for existence. (In *4-Sided Triangle* a duplicating machine; in *Voyage* an alternate, identical universe.)

At the moment, and despite *2001*, sf film and sf literature are still distinctly different genres, but there now seems opportunity for them to draw closer and derive strength from one another. Now most sf stories take place in the future and most sf films in the present, not only because of the traditionally limited budget for the sf flick but because directors and designers have been too unimaginative to come up with interesting new surfaces. What to look at has been one of the hardest problems for sf. Verne predicted the periscope; Cleve Cartmill predicted the atomic bomb; Poe predicted the computer. But who could have predicted Andy Warhol or Larry Zox or Claes Oldenburg?

2001: A Space Odyssey

It's the surface of things which stymies the imagination. As a species of rarefied talk, sf could go on forever, always more involuted, always more derivative. But the fact that Kubrick and Fellini, with his *Satyricon*, were able to produce surfaces, and even textures, for their imagined worlds ought to inspire the sf writers to come more straightforwardly at their themes and characters. Maybe we will even get a sf novel with odors and tastes in it. . . . **Conversely, it is imperative to remark that *2001* and *Satyricon* are beginnings and not endings, and that sf film makers — *after* they have effected a visual surface for the future or for Mars —may begin to deal a bit with some of the ideas that are the stock in trade of the literature.**

Hope for the best.
But knock on wood.

It Came from Outer Space

THE ALIEN LANDSCAPES OF THE PLANET EARTH:

SCIENCE FICTION IN THE FIFTIES

Vivian Sobchack

Men standing in a circle on a vast field of ice. Strange inhuman footprints on an impressionable beach. A little girl stiffly walking in the desert. Giant crystalline rocks toppling over themselves in an arid wasteland. A barren and craggy seacoast where in a cave an alien thing waits.

These are the gray images of the low-budget science fiction film that stay in the mind, clear and — to this day — chilling. The rockets and space stations and Interociter-like gadgetry in the science fiction films of the fifties and early sixties seem like the artifacts of some quaintly primitive civilization when they are placed beside the technological realizations in films like *2001: A Space Odyssey*, *Marooned* and *Silent Running*. Yet even these latter marvels of special effects and wondrous set design will — on the basis of their gadgetry — suffer the ravages of time and technological actuality. If they are to be remembered, their lasting value will rest on elements far removed from the atmosphere of scientific accuracy currently evoked by their backgrounds. What we wonder at today, we may laugh at tomorrow.

But the desert and the beach, the wind and the sea, the black lagoon and the frozen stretches of Arctic ice do not date, and will

49 /

never lose their power to awe and disturb us. Tied to limited budgets, imaginative filmmakers like Jack Arnold, John Sherwood and Gordon Douglas found themselves earthbound, grounded. But unlike those directors who feebly and laughably tried to imitate the more expensive spectaculars with a one room, one dial set, Arnold and the others set out to discover a new world with which to amaze us, one comparable to the vast reaches of outer space in its capacity to evoke wonder; the world they discovered was Earth. Financial necessity kept them on the ground, but imagination drove them to use the landscapes of our own planet as alien terrain.

Their very inability to reach for the stars created in films like *The Space Children*, *The Monolith Monsters* and *Them!* a new vision of Earth and, as a result, a new vision of Man. Forever on the ground, they gave us those lasting and pessimistic images of Man confronting the void here on Earth.

The cold vastness of impersonal space, the terror of Man confronting the universe and the void — out there — has always been largely neutralized in the more expensively-mounted space exploration films which have been popular since the fifties. In movies like *Destination Moon*, *Riders to the Stars*, *The Conquest of Space*, Man has always slipped into his rocket as though it were a new automobile. His jargon has been reassuring; his technological accomplishments, banal competence, and Tom Swiftian enthusiasm has — within the protective armor of his starship — robbed the infinite of its ability to really terrify us, reduced its blank impenetrability to the dimensions of a highway.

2001: A Space Odyssey is perhaps the only exception; in its third segment, it actually — dizzyingly — evokes a real sense of an incomprehensible void. Underlying all the other films, however, is the smug idea that all earthly terrain has been challenged and conquered and that there is nowhere to go but — literally and metaphorically — up. Implicit in the image of a sleek silvered rocketship surrounded by a blackness bejeweled with stars is both the optimistic belief in infinite human and technological progress and a view of the void as a beautiful undiscovered country (no neighbor to Hamlet's) which holds only minor terrors because it is, in fact, ultimately discoverable, conquerable.

Those films which take us "out there" into space or to other planets are — no matter how dour their warnings against nuclear war or the dangers of creeping intellectualism — essentially optimistic. They show Man as conqueror, Earth as home. They are reassuring not merely because what happens occurs "out there." It is not simply that war on another planet is more palatable than war here, that alien invasion into our territory is more insupportable than our intrusion elsewhere, or that monsters and mutants light years away are less immediately threatening than if they are actually stomping our cities, eating our brains, and lusting after our women. What is reassuring and optimistic about these films is their very view of the alien and strange as something other, something apart and separate from Man and his personal and private domain, *our* planet.

This optimism based on the very definite distinction between the known and the unknown also found its way to earthly battlefields in extravaganzas like *The War of the Worlds, Twenty Million Miles to Earth,* even *The Andromeda Strain*, but Earth itself was on our side. All humanity and the "fate of the planet" itself (assumed here is some unstated symbiotic relationship) was threatened, and threatened here rather than there, but we still had a definite sense of identity which gave us spiritual strength. We saw the threat as "them" or "it" — the alien as separate from ourselves and the ground beneath our feet. We knew who we were in these films and we knew what our world was. Earth and Man were an organic unit, a known quantity, working together to repel the alien "other." Our cities and traffic and technology, our churches and monuments gave an anthropomorphic — and therefore reassuring — face to our planet. These movies suggested that we and the very ground we walked upon were intimately bound together, harmoniously entwined in some metaphysical lovers' embrace.

At the same time these films that celebrated Man and his works and the whole concept of infinite possibility were being made, those imaginative and financially-hampered filmmakers previously mentioned were quietly, grayly, pessimistically pulling the ground out from beneath our complacent feet. In their films, Man's previously harmonious marriage to the terrain of our planet ended in divorce. These directors (and particularly Jack Arnold) removed the anthropomorphic physiognomy of cities and tilled land from their images. The Earth — our hitherto known and beloved planet — itself became alien, unknown and, most terrifying of all, hostile. In a search for cheap locations, these filmmakers discovered the desert and the beach — empty and supposedly neutral backgrounds which could admit more easily than could the city and town the introduction of the extraordinary and the fantastic into what was, after all, a real and familiar world. What happens in their films, however, is that the extraordinary and the fantastic — the monsters and mutants and alien invaders — become almost secondary in their ability to evoke awe and fear in the audience. What creates the terrifying wonder and hopelessness in their films is not the giant ant or spider, not the creature, not the alien invader in what- ever form he appears, but the terrain of Earth itself.

Viewing those dark and brooding seascapes, the dull wet sand and the surf crashing crazily against the outrageous and indefinable geometry of towering rocks, seeing the unshadowed and limitless stretches of desert punctuated by the stiff and inhuman form of an occasional cactus or the frantic scurrying of some tiny and vulner- able rodent, the spectator is forced to a recognition, however un- conscious it may remain, of Man's precarious condition, his vul- nerability "right here" as well as "out there" to the void, his total isolation, the fragile quality of his body and his works, the terrifying blankness in the eyes of what he thought was Mother Nature.

The desert and the beach — as opposed to those imaginary worlds created on a studio set or in the laboratory — do exist, are real. When they become the receptive breeding ground or hiding place for those things which threaten to destroy us, they threaten to destroy us as well. Working inversely from those movies which optimistically reduce the infinitudes and uncertainties of space to a view seen from an intergalactic automobile, the films which show us the "other-ness" of the world in which we actually live expand the finite and certain limits of a car on a highway winding through a desert or along a lonely stretch of seacoast into a journey through an infinite and terrifying void. When the land which has seemed a part of us threatens us, we are truly lost in space.

The desert and the sea certainly have always been somewhat strange to us, but they have not been inordinately malevolent. They are unfamiliar, yet familiar, areas of our world and are full of mythic significance which we usually do not care to contemplate in our entertainments. To bring in Freud or Jung here would not be out of place. But on a conscious level, we have attempted to reduce the strangeness of these places, reduce their size: the desert to a mere space between cities, the sea to a resort area. We have found a certain illusory security in the existence of Las Vegas, in the belief that we can make the desert bloom if we choose to. Despite our ecologically-concerned expressions of horror at a beach strewn with beer cans and plastic sandwich wrap, one can see in this littering the small and puny attempt to make a human impression of a threateningly empty terrain.

What such films as *It Came from Outer Space, Them!, Tarantula, The Creature from the Black Lagoon* and *The Space Children* tell us is that we cannot make an impression on the Earth. It is not only a part of us; it does not even recognize us. These films take us away from our larger structures, our skyscrapers and cities which break up the disturbing regularity of the horizon. Even *Them!* which partially seems an exception because we move from the desert to Los Angeles for the second portion of the film is consistent in its destruction of the familiar. We enter a mental hospital, see a forgotten and deserted area of the city, and quickly go underground into storm drains which appear labyrinthine and menacing, not just because the giant ants are hiding there but also because the very city rests not on solid ground, on instead a series of tunnels which might collapse at any time. Usually, however, we are removed from the city. Our civilization and its technological apparatus is at best a small town set on the edge of an abyss, set against an unbroken horizon. Watching the images of these films, their insistence on a fathomless landscape, we are forced to a pessimistic view of technological progress and Man's ability to control his destiny. We are constantly shown human beings set against the agelessness of the desert and the sea. We are always reminded that the land and the water were here before us and will be here long after we are gone. Man looks puny and incredibly mortal against the unblinking and bare landscapes we see.

In *It Came from Outer Space,* the camera scans a desert in which a row of telephone poles and the men working on the wires appear ineffectual in breaking up the endless wasteland and the empty sky. The men doing their jobs, trying to impose order and limits on an expressionless and terrifying expanse of space, seem to unconsciously recognize the futility of their attempt. One of them voices the uncertainty and discomfort we all must deal with: "You see lakes and rivers that aren't really there, and sometimes you think the wind gets into the wires and sings to itself." The land is deceptive and the wind sings, not to Man, but to itself.

The giant ants in *Them!* may have been the result of Man's power to split the atom, but it is the desert which nurtures and

Them!

protects the mutants. Their nest is there, unidentifiable and hidden except when seen from above by helicopter. A sandstorm separates the human characters from each other in their initial inquiry and makes them vulnerable to the first attack we see on the screen. People hear strange noises, fatalistically shrug their shoulders, and say that the wind is "pretty freakish" in and around the desert; the wind, too, has changed and become a freakish mutant. The force of the ants is seen as no less fierce than the force of the elements. Man in comparison is weak. It is interesting that in so many of these films human beings are shown as transients, not even strong enough to set up permanent dwellings on the hostile land. The little girl who has stumbled off the desert in shock and her family were living not in a house, but in a trailer. The general store which is broken into is rickety, made of wood, full of cracks; one can hear the wind blowing through the chinks in its poor armor and see the sand insinuating its way in to coat the counters and the floor.

Tarantula, too, removes us from the small and questionable stability of a town and takes us to a house totally isolated in the desert. The house, once seen, is immediately doomed; it cannot possibly survive against so straight a horizon. In one scene a man and a woman stand in the desert, minute against a wide fathomless sky and an ungeometric, uncivilized, outcropping of rocks. Both are scientists: he a doctor, she a biologist. Yet lines like "Everything that ever crept or crawled the earth once lived here," "It's quiet yet strangely evil, as if it were hiding its secret from man," and "You can't second-guess the desert" — despite their absurdly reductive use of language — express something terrifying when heard against the image of the rocks and waste and sky and the suddenly ridiculous automobile parked diminutively by the side of a quasi-road.

In *The Creature from the Black Lagoon* we are not even offered the small and fragile security of a community. Rather than living at the edge of an abyss, the characters are floating on it. The waters of the lagoon are deceptively quiet, shimmeringly beautiful and clear, but subsequently reveal themselves as black, opaque, unfathomable and hostile — nurturing a "creature" and rejecting man. Although the Creature is eventually wounded, he is not really

The Creature from the Black Lagoon

shown to be mortal in his own territory. The Lagoon is his world and no part of ours. Here it might be interesting to note that as long as the "other" is on the desert, on the beach, or in the water he is almost always indestructible. As long as he is connected with the landscape which supports him, Man cannot successfully subdue him. That previously anthropomorphic union between Man and his physical environment has been changed to show a union of hostile forces. Man can only conquer in his own small enclaves. The giant ants are killed in city drains, not on the desert; the "Thing" is electrocuted indoors, not destroyed on the frozen wasteland of Arctic ice; the alien power in *The Space Children* can return, unharmed, to whence it came since it has made no move to leave the cave on the beach; the Creature is still safe as long as he remains in the Lagoon.

This alien earthly landscape is powerfully evoked in *The Space Children*, an Arnold film which is a bit logically inoperative and, therefore, often dismissed and not often seen. A rocky seacoast and beach protect an alien power (something which starts out as a glowing pebble and grows into a ridiculously glowing brain). Only the children in the area know of it and it telepathically commands them to sabotage a missile on the military base at which their parents work. The power is more laugh-provoking than it is terrifying. What is terrifying, however, is the landscape. Only the children in the film possess any positive connection with the desolate environment, unaware of the implications of its frightening limitlessness. And yet even they are constantly seen clutching sweaters, picking up jackets, protecting themselves against some chilling wind. Their parents are hopelessly and ineffectually seen trying to impress their presence on the landscape but they are unsuccessful and voice their uneasiness frequently. They live in little mobile homes, a tiny trailer park on the brink of infinity. And a traditional barbecue becomes — against the bleakness of the terrain and the blackness of night — one of the saddest and most futile of human activities. Even before it is broken up by human hostility, it is only the smallest candle lit against the chaotic and incomprehensible void here on Earth.

The Thing from Another World

Films using the land of Earth as negative and hostile have been made in places other than the desert and the beach although not as frequently. The Arctic has effectually given us the frozen and hostile world of *The Thing* as well as the setting for the chilling discovery of the Rhedosaurus in *The Beast from 20,000 Fathoms*. The swamp and the jungle have threatened us much less effec-

/ 58

It Came from Outer Space

tively, however, because they have not been particularly useful in evoking that sense of the void which gives the low-budget film its particularly devastating quality. The swamp and the jungle — however alien to those of us who are used to pavement beneath our feet — are too leafy, too obstructed and constricted, and do not allow us that sense of unconfinable and unconquerable space that is associated with the desert and the sea and the Arctic, that sense of rootlessness and impermanence which terrifies us all.

The science fiction film has come into its own again after a slack period. *2001* has made it respectable and, to some, profound. But those filmmakers who would continue in the wake of big-budget extravaganzas might well bear in mind that there is nothing quite like unpaved earth and endless horizon for expressing the infinite.

INVASION OF
THE BODY SNATCHERS:
A CLASSIC OF SUBTLE HORROR

Stuart M. Kaminsky

There are no moments of great violence in *Invasion of the Body Snatchers*. We see no one die on screen (and, technically, no one dies in the film). There are no monsters and few special effects. The special effects are confined totally to the construction of a few pods shown only briefly. The essence of *Invasion of the Body Snatchers*, directed by Don Siegel in 1956, is its aura of normalcy. It is normalcy, the acceptance of the status quo, the desire to escape from the pain of the abnormal that creates the sense of horror in the film.

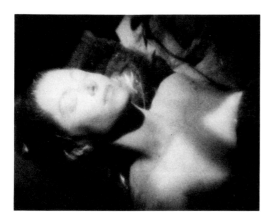

A pod assuming
human shape

One problem in dealing with the film is the frame, the prologue and epilogue. The film, as released, opens with Dr. Miles Bennell in a hospital claiming to an incredulous psychiatrist (played by Whit Bissell) that creatures from outer space have taken over the town of Santa Mira, California. Miles (Kevin McCarthy) tells his story of the pod take-over which we see in flashback with Miles' voice narrating at the start. The film ends with Miles concluding his story to the psychiatrist who appears on the verge of having him taken away. At the critical moment another physician says that a man has been killed driving a truck filled with strange pods. The psychiatrist believes Miles and the film ends with the doctor on the phone asking for the F.B.I.

The problem with the opening and closing sections just discussed is similar to that of the frame sections of *The Cabinet of Dr. Caligari* (1919) in which a madman tells a story and then we return to him in the hospital. Don Siegel, after completing *Invasion of the Body Snatchers*, did not want the frame, nor did his writer Daniel Mainwaring, according to discussions I have had with them both. By the same token, the writers of *The Cabinet of Dr. Caligari* were opposed to the frame. In both cases, the objection was that the frame offered an out, a possible note of affirmation whereas they saw their films as deeply pessimistic.

Mainwaring wrote the frame sequences after Allied Artists' executives previewed the film and decided that audiences did not understand the plot. Siegel reluctantly directed the frame sequences knowing that another director would be called in to do them if he refused. Says screenwriter Daniel Mainwaring (pronounced mainwere): "The frame was added after several bad previews. The audiences — bad ones — couldn't understand the film and because the Mirisches threatened to bring in another director and writer to make changes, I made the changes and convinced Don, against his will, to shoot them. I did it because I didn't want a stranger completely screwing up our work."

My primary objection to the frame is that it blunts the conclusion. The film, as Siegel wanted it, was to end with McCarthy on the highway unable to get anyone to listen to his story of the pod take-over and turning to the camera to shout, "You're next!"

Becky's father descends stairs as Kaufman, Jack, and Miles
discuss body discovered earlier in cellar

Miles, Becky, and her Aunt Wilma speculate that
Uncle Ira may not be Uncle Ira

Citizens of Santa Mira gather to spread pods to other towns

The moment would be a powerful warning, a psychological assault. However the conclusion of the film as it stands is still not totally affirmative, which is as it should be. We have seen the pods in action. We know they have already begun to spread. We wonder if human effort — the F.B.I. — can really have any effect. In addition, up to the moment Bissell picks up the phone, the possibility remains in the back of our minds that he may be a pod. In fact, the film has, at that point, so powerfully established a sense of mistrust for appearances that we are relieved with McCarthy when the doctor proves to be human. If there is any weakness in this it is that McCarthy does not appear, in the frame, to have this deep distrust of the doctor that we have developed.

A great deal of the power of the film comes in the visual presentation of the town of Santa Mira. Everything looks normal. Everyone acts normal even when they are not. Somehow, and Siegel himself isn't always sure how he managed it, there is something slightly off in the pod people. As one character, Wilma, puts it in talking about her Uncle Ira, there is no real emotion, just the pretense of it.

*Miles and Becky hide in
mine cave to escape mob
of pursuing citizens*

As we grow more absorbed in the film, we gradually begin to view the normal as ominous. That is, indeed, the basis of the theme of the film and a perfect wedding of style and content. Conformity, acceptance, control of emotions are the norm. It is this control, in fact, the very lack of feeling which is the horror of pod-ism. Pod-ism in the film involves the process of one's mind and thoughts being absorbed in a duplicate body which grows from a pod. The pod is emotionless and being so is also invulnerable. The parallel is clear but not heavy. Siegel fears that the pressures of existence are driving man into a shell, turning him into a vegetable creature who cannot feel, only give the pretense of feeling. That, to Siegel, is equivalent to being dead. In the film, one turns into a pod when he goes to sleep. Becoming a pod is like dying. Becoming a figurative pod is like being emotionally dead.

Again, a power of the film is its ambiguity. While being a pod is repugnant to Siegel and, in the film, to McCarthy, the argument for accepting pod-ism is strong.

First, there are many references to the forces in the world driving man into the defense of a pod existence.

McCarthy tells Wilma (Virginia Christine) that she is not mad. "Even these days," he says, "it's not as easy to go crazy as you think." The implication is that "these days" are frightening, fearful, something from which one might well wish to escape in madness.

Later, when McCarthy thinks the pod reports are examples of mass hysteria, he asks a psychiatrist, Danny Kaufman (Larry Gates) what causes it. "Worry about what's going on in the world, probably," says Kaufman.

When Becky Driscoll (Dana Wynter) and McCarthy begin to believe in the existence of the pods, she asks him for an explanation and he responds, "So much has been discovered in the past ten years."

Overtly, he is referring to scientific discoveries, even to the atomic bomb. Additionally, he is saying that the very existence of such threats is an overwhelming weight on man.

The one hint of feeling on the part of a pod is particularly enlightening in the film. McCarthy sneaks up to the house of his nurse and listens at the window. He hears the nurse, Sally (Jean Willes) tell someone where to put a pod for her baby. When the baby wakes up, she says, "there will be no more tears." Clearly, the pods are bringing comfort, a retreat from pain and life, a state of total emotional tranquility.

After hiding the night in McCarthy's office, he and Dana Wynter look out the window to see the town square. From their point of view it looks normal. The people look normal, but by now we distrust the normal as they do and we are confirmed. The trucks begin to pull out with pods, taking them to other communities. The third truck goes to Milltown and the reference again is to the spread of a state of tranquility. Yet McCarthy says, "It's a malignant disease spreading through the whole country."

It is at this point that McCarthy makes the thematic statement central to the film: "Only when we have to fight to stay human do we realize how precious our humanity is." Humanity, he explains, drains away without our knowing it and we are suddenly dead.

It is in the conversation with the pod psychiatrist, Gates, that the ambiguity is most clearly expressed. In interviews (with the author and with Peter Bogdanovich in Movie #15) Siegel has shown that he has mixed feelings about the actual state of pod-ism, the masking, killing of emotion and subjugation of one's pain to a state of meaningless nirvana. Acceptance of pod-ism means the elimination of the fear of death and pain. As Gates points out, a pod has "no need for love, emotions." There is also no need for fear. Gates is reasonable, his argument rational and convincing. McCarthy's final response is that the world of the pods is one "where everyone is the same." For all its pain and fear, existence to him is worth fighting for. It is the only thing that makes his life meaningful. There is no essential difference between being a pod and being dead. And yet, death is inevitable and the pod state makes that death easier to accept and this life easier to bear. The dilemma drives McCarthy to the edge of madness for his whole world converts to pod-ism, just as one's real world dies around him. Santa Mira is an enclosed town, surrounded by mountains. When he arrives at the beginning, McCarthy says he feels like a stranger in his own country. Indeed, his friends, patients, colleagues and the girl he loves succumb to the inevitability of the pod takeover. It takes an extraordinary act of will and determination for McCarthy to stay awake. One has to fight for one's humanity. It is easy to become a pod.

The universality of the theme and the power of its presentation in the genre of a science fiction/horror context can be seen in two films by directors who very much admire Siegel. In Jean Luc Godard's *Alphaville* (1965) the threat is the computer, the pod-like state is that of giving one's self over to the mechanistic, the proscribed. In *Alphaville*, existence is too much for man and he turns his mind over to the computer. One scene in the Godard film in fact is directly taken from the Siegel film. Anna Karina and Eddie Constantine must show no emotion when they see a man killed. To show emotion is to indicate that you are not in the power of the computer. They reveal themselves and have a difficult time escaping. When McCarthy and Miss Wynter leave his office to try to escape, he tells her to look blank, show no emotion. She sees a dog about to be hit by a car and she reveals herself. It is, by the way, interesting to note that Siegel vividly remembers an incident more than twenty years ago when he saw a dog about to be hit by a car and could not get himself to react to save the animal.

The second director influenced by Siegel's film was François Truffaut. In *Fahrenheit 451* (1966), the people are literally tranquilized with drugs. They are dull, content. Books are forbidden because they create emotional responses which, as the pods informed us, are harmful. It is Montag's supreme effort to feel that allows him to reject his wife, promotion, security and, like McCarthy and Constantine, to spend his life running.

The thematic goals of *Invasion of the Body Snatchers* are beautifully expressed in content (the dialogue primarily) and style (the visual body).

The fact that one cannot escape from the pods is shown by Siegel in the way he has the pods hidden before they take over the minds of the humans. We see them in basements, automobile trunks, a greenhouse, and on a home pool table. That they cannot be destroyed is shown in McCarthy's attempts to do so. When he discovers the pods growing in the greenhouse, we are shown a ritual vampire killing. The camera is low in the point of view of the pod. We see McCarthy's anguished face as he drives the pitchfork down and leaves it like a stake through the heart. But it is not enough. Other pods appear in his trunk. He burns them in much the way we have seen so many monsters burning in films (only to rise again in a sequel). The pods are not traditional terrors. They are modern terrors not to be destroyed. There is no catharsis in the presentation of a monster being destroyed by love or religious ritual. It is the monsters which keep rising to prevail.

That he expects his warning not to be heeded is shown by Siegel in a variety of ways. Perhaps the most striking is that of the use of the small boy, Jimmy Grimaldi, whom we meet with McCarthy at the beginning of the picture. He runs down the road and is stopped by McCarthy whom he informs that his mother is not his mother. McCarthy doesn't believe him. The world will not believe him and eventually the boy becomes a pod. Late in the film we also see McCarthy running down the road, searching for someone to tell that the people of Santa Mira are not really the people of

Santa Mira (the very name of the town — mira in Spanish means "look" — calls attention to itself, cries to be understood, heeded). Like Jimmy, we know McCarthy will not be believed.

In the film McCarthy is constantly being driven into dark corners, forced to hide, his world threatened by the pods, reduced to constricted areas of existence. In one case, he and Dana Wynter have to hide in a closet in his office. The camera moves with them into the closet and through a small hole in the door we see a pod turn on a light outside. Later McCarthy and Miss Wynter are forced to hide in a cave in a hole which they cover with boards. They bury themselves. We see the pods rush over them. In effect, the places to run are constantly reduced and we suffer the confinement of choices with the protagonists.

The most striking sequence in the film for me is that in which McCarthy, having finally escaped from Santa Mira, suddenly finds himself on a highway with hundreds of cars passing him, unwilling to listen to him, unwilling to save themselves. The setting is dark with McCarthy frantic in a sea of machines, people hiding within their machines, perhaps in the first step of becoming pods.

As he stands on the highway, a truck passes with the names of various cities on it. In the truck, McCarthy finds the pods and we know they are being taken to the big cities whose names we saw on the side of the truck. We feel as hopeless in the face of the image as McCarthy.

In final scene, hero sees truckloads of pods being transported to other cities

Finally, an important contribution to the total power of the film lies in the performances. McCarthy's growing frenzy combined with his determination never falter. A less restrained actor might well have been a disaster. The other actors have the burden of appearing normal while at the same time conveying the impression that they are not. It is in the performances that this ambiguity is carried. Siegel seldom relies on low key lighting, ominous shadows or radical camera angles or shock cutting to carry the terror of the situation. It is in the very matter-of-factness of presentation that the film holds its power and it is Siegel's handling of actors which contributes considerably to the film which Leslie Halliwell in *The Filmgoer's Companion* calls "the most subtle film in the science-fiction cycle, with no visual horror whatever."

DON SIEGEL ON
THE POD SOCIETY

Stuart M. Kaminsky

Although *Invasion of the Body Snatchers* (1956) is considered one of the most intelligent science fiction films ever made, it is unique in Siegel's 28-film career. He has not directed another science fiction film nor seriously considered doing one. He did, however, direct two episodes of the *Twilight Zone* television series, "Uncle Simon" (11/15/63) starring Sir Cedric Hardwicke and Constance Ford, and "The Self-Improvement of Salvadore Ross" (1/17/64) starring Don Gordon. Both episodes were written by Rod Serling.

Of all his films, *Invasion of the Body Snatchers* is the one most central to Siegel's thematic interests. It is the film about which he most frequently talks when discussing his attitudes toward life, and the term "pod" — a reference to the pod creatures of the film — is part of his normal vocabulary.

The film was initially the idea of Walter Wanger, the producer, who had read Jack Finney's novel (originally published as a magazine series) and brought the idea to Siegel who immediately liked it. Siegel got Daniel Mainwaring to write the screenplay, Ted Haworth as art director and Kevin McCarthy as star.

73 /

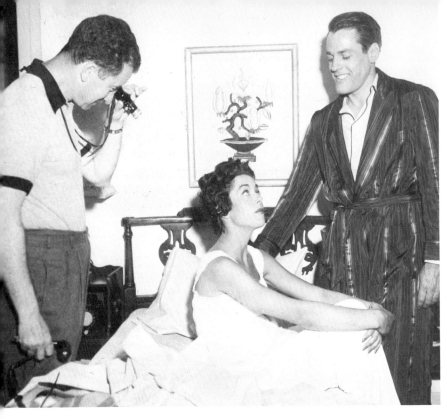

Don Siegel (at left) with Dana Wynter and Kevin
McCarthy during filming of **Invasion of the
Body Snatchers**

Don Siegel (left) uses Kevin McCarthy to
demonstrate proper way of fighting pods played by
Ralph Dumke, Larry Gates, and King Donovan

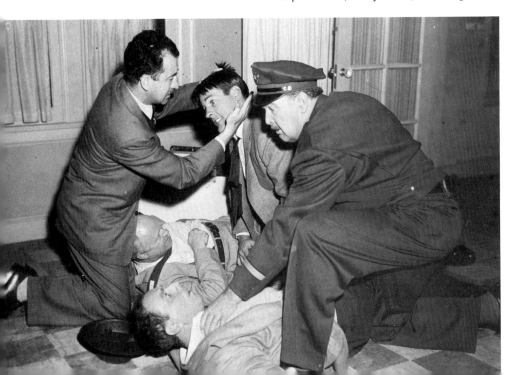

The following interview with Siegel was obtained while gathering material for a book on Siegel and his work. As background, Siegel was born in Chicago but moved frequently with his family throughout his youth. At one point, he attended Cambridge University when his family moved to Europe where his father was sent to manage an American business in Paris. At the age of 19, Siegel got a job on an ocean liner, made his way across the United States and found himself in Los Angeles where he managed to get an interview at Warner Bros. with Hal Wallis. Wallis gave him a job at the bottom of the editing echelon. Through the 1930s Siegel worked as a film librarian, film editor, montage director and second unit director on dozens of films including *Sergeant York, Saratoga Trunk,* and *The Roaring Twenties.* For much of his time at Warner (he left in 1945) he worked under Byron Haskin.

Siegel became a director in 1945 with *The Verdict* and has, among his directing credits, *Riot in Cell Block 11, Baby Face Nelson, Madigan, Two Mules for Sister Sarah, Hell is for Heroes, Coogan's Bluff, Dirty Harry, The Killers* and, my own favorite, *The Beguiled.*

KAMINSKY: It has been reported that Sam Peckinpah wrote a script for or part of *Invasion of the Body Snatchers.* Is that true?

SIEGEL: No. Sam was my assistant on that picture, as he was on several of my pictures including *Riot in Cell Block 11* and *Private Hell 36.* Sam may have made suggestions, but he didn't write any of the film. Sam did act in the film, however. He was one of the pods, the meter reader in Dana Wynter's basement.

KAMINSKY: The film has a frame, a prologue and epilogue which shows Kevin McCarthy being brought into a hospital to tell his story and then later, at the end, getting the doctor to believe him when some pods are found. According to Daniel Mainwaring you were very much against the frame.

SIEGEL: Very much against it. Danny wrote it because they told him he had to.

KAMINSKY: "They?"

SIEGEL: The studio.

KAMINSKY: Did you direct the prologue and epilogue?

SIEGEL: Yes. They were going to shoot it anyway and I decided that since it would be in the picture, I might as well do it as well as I could.

KAMINSKY: What don't you like about the prologue and epilogue?

SIEGEL: First of all, it lets you know right away that something unusual is going on. If you start, as I wanted to, with McCarthy arriving in the town of Santa Mira, it reveals itself slowly, we understand why McCarthy can't readily accept the terrible thing that appears to be happening. And the dramatic impact of the ending is reduced with the epilogue. I wanted to end it with McCarthy on the highway turning to the camera and saying, "You're next!" Then, boom, the lights go up. In the final version, however, we go back to the hospital . . . and that's after the fact.

KAMINSKY: The film is still extremely popular. According to NTA, which distributes it, it is among the most requested films on television. Can't the opening and close be cut or is my question naive?

SIEGEL: Many people do cut that frame, those sequences, when they show it. Every few days the picture is run somewhere, some underground theater. And the tacked on opening and closing are removed.

KAMINSKY: Do you think anything else hurt the film?

SIEGEL: Yes. Allied Artists had an old-fashioned credo that horror pictures couldn't have humor. I had a great deal of humor in the picture and though they cut out a lot, they didn't totally succeed.

KAMINSKY: What was the basis of the humor they cut out?

SIEGEL: I felt that the idea of pods growing into a likeness of a person would strike the characters as preposterous. I wanted to play it that way, with the characters not taking the threat seriously. For example, if you told me now that there was a pod in my likeness in the other room, I would joke about it. However, when I opened the door and saw the pod, the full shock and horror would hit me and the fun would be gone. I wanted the people in the film to behave like normal people. That does come through in the film.

KAMINSKY: As in the barbecue scene. King Donovan, Carolyn Jones, McCarthy and Dana Wynter have an outdoor barbecue even after they have accepted mentally that something is terribly wrong. Only when they see the pod do they panic.

SIEGEL: Precisely.

KAMINSKY: The film contains surprisingly few special effects, surprising because your background at Warner Bros. was in montage and effects.

SIEGEL: Well, special effects were relatively unimportant in *Invasion of the Body Snatchers*. We spent about $15,000 on special effects, a very small amount. Instead of doing what so many science fiction and horror films do . . . spend all their money on special effects and put poor actors on the screen . . . we concentrated on the performers. The main thing about the picture, however, was that it was about something and that's rare.

KAMINSKY: It's about . . .

SIEGEL: Pods. Not those that come from outer space, vegetables from outer space. People are pods. Many of my associates are certainly pods. They have no feelings. They exist, breathe, sleep. To be a pod means that you have no passion, no anger, the spark has left you.

KAMINSKY: Your spokesman for the pods is a psychiatrist played by Larry Gates. A psychiatrist in the real world usually represents sanity and . . .

SIEGEL: Having the psychiatrist as spokesman for the pods was a conscious choice. Once you become a pod you believe in it and he really believes in it, is able to speak with authority, knowledge about how it is preferable to be a pod instead of a human.

KAMINSKY: Yes, you allow him to make a frighteningly strong case for accepting pod-ism.

SIEGEL: Well, I think there's a very strong case for being a pod. These pods, who get rid of pain, ill health and mental disturbance are, in a sense, doing good. It happens to leave you with a very dull world, but that, by the way, my dear friend, is the world that most of us live in. It's the same as people who welcome going into the army or prison. There's regimentation, a lack of having to make up your mind, face decisions.

KAMINSKY: So one point of the picture is that being a pod relieves you but gives you no challenge. To be a pod is the same as not existing.

SIEGEL: That's right.

KAMINSKY: In *Invasion of the Body Snatchers,* there is no real physical threat from the pods. The threat is from sleep. Sleep is the villain. To fall asleep is to allow the pods to take your mind.

SIEGEL: Yes. It's a very frightening thing to face, the physical challenge of keeping someone awake. The suspense created is very great because, obviously, we'll all have to sleep. It's like when people suffer from chronic insomnia as I do. They are afraid to go to sleep. One reason for this is that they fear they won't wake up. There is a parallel to this in the film.

KAMINSKY: When McCarthy meets Dana Wynter on his return to Santa Mira, he invites her to go somewhere with him. He jokingly says, "It's summer, the moon is full and I know a bank where the wild thyme grows." It is one of many motifs picked up and played with from more traditional horror films. When McCarthy does encounter the pods, he tries all the traditional ways to kill them, though it is not underscored. In the greenhouse, you made a special point of having the camera down low when he plunges a pitchfork into the pod, like driving a stake through the heart. And later he tries to burn the pods placed in his trunk.

SIEGEL: But more appear.

KAMINSKY: The only thing he can do is run and even that . . .

SIEGEL: . . . he can't do. He tries to get the police on his side but he discovers that the police are pods. He tries to call Washington but discovers the telephone operator is a pod. He can only try to escape.

KAMINSKY: We get quite far into the film before we and McCarthy are absolutely sure the pods exist.

SIEGEL: That's right. We delayed it as long as we could because from that moment on, it was just an out-and-out chase, the whole town against this one person who isn't a pod and this girl who isn't one but will be. What I thought was quite delicious was the fact that pods feel no passion. So after he comes back to her in the cave and kisses her to keep her awake, a delicious, non-pod kiss, he knows she's a pod because she's a limp fish.

KAMINSKY: By the way, do you like the title of the picture?

SIEGEL: No. *Invasion of the Body Snatchers* was the idea of some studio pod. The title I wanted was *Sleep No More*.

KAMINSKY: Referring to Hamlet's soliloquy on suicide?

SIEGEL: Yes.

KAMINSKY: The reason McCarthy leaves her in the cave is because he hears music, Brahms I believe, although the script originally called for Mexican music. In any case, it makes him think it is being played by real people because pods have no need for music.

SIEGEL: And he finds they are pods waiting for the weather forecast while they load more pods on a truck. I frequently try to mislead the audience a little.

KAMINSKY: That's especially jarring since the doctor, McCarthy, has gotten to the point where he trusts almost no one. At the end, this distrust pushes him to the brink of madness.

SIEGEL: Well, there he is on the highway, trying to get someone to listen to his warning and no one will listen. It would probably drive you crazy. Remember he spins against a truck, tries to climb in and sees that it is filled with pods going to all the different cities marked on the side of the truck. That's when he wheels around and yells "You're next!" Because you are next. I don't care where you are, whether you're sitting in a theatre or reading a magazine, whether you are in the United States or another country. There are pods and they are going to get you.

KAMINSKY: At one point when the pods are being disbursed from trucks in the town square, we hear that one is for the people of Milltown. Was this one of the jokes, a comment of some kind on tranquilizing one's self into pod-ism?

SIEGEL: Well, that was in the script. It's possible we meant it as a gag, but I don't remember.

KAMINSKY: Everything about the film is constricting, closed in on itself. We see little Jimmy Grimaldi running down the road away from his pod mother at the beginning of the picture and later we see McCarthy running in the same kind of panic down the same road when he is pursued by the pods.

/ 80

SIEGEL: That was done quite deliberately. I like that. In many of my pictures, I'll start with some action and later end with a related action, an action related in style.

KAMINSKY: Then there are some intangible things that make the film particularly chilling. For example, Uncle Ira played by Tom Fadden is particularly frightening although he does nothing but mow the lawn while the girl whispers that he is not her Uncle Ira. Now the camera position and lighting are important, but there's something else.

SIEGEL: Perhaps his face. The fact that he's older than he looks might have done something. I remember working with him on the scene and being very pleased with the way it came off. Part of it was a strange little smile he gave.

KAMINSKY: Yes. It is normal and yet something is wrong. People are not who you think them to be and, ultimately, your greatest enemy is your own pod self. There are many references to fear of one's self. It is especially striking when King Donovan goes off with Carolyn Jones and says to McCarthy "Look out for yourself." It is a bit of commonplace banter, but we know that it is chillingly literal. Ultimately it is our own tendency toward pod-ism which we must overcome.

SIEGEL: Yes, I don't think you're reading anything that isn't there.

KAMINSKY: As far as McCarthy being a doctor . . .

SIEGEL: The town is like a cancer growth. The town, like a section of your body, is ill, and it's going to spread, the way, many times, political ideas spread.

KAMINSKY: There are some parallels in the film to Howard Hawks' *The Thing*, which came before *Invasion of the Body Snatchers* and dealt with an emotionless vegetable creature from outer space that lived off humans and, more recently, to *Night of the Living Dead* in which the metaphor becomes most stark and those who die become pods consuming the living and . . .

SIEGEL: . . . there was a television series, *The Invaders* which was along the same lines.

KAMINSKY: That's right. Creatures from outer space replacing humans, and if I might add, it's the theme of Godard's *Alphaville* in which people become podlike and give themselves over to a computer. Have you ever seen the film?

SIEGEL: No.

KAMINSKY: What we come back to is that there is no hope in your film.

SIEGEL: People without being vegetables are becoming vegetables. I don't know what the answer is except an awareness of it. That's what makes a picture like *Invasion of the Body Snatchers* important.

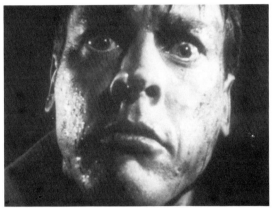

Becky falls asleep and becomes a pod

SOLARIS:
A CONTEMPORARY MASTERPIECE

Lee Atwell

The electric confluence of revolution and poetry sustained in the films of Eisenstein, Pudovkin, Dovzhenko, and Vertov, during those brief, optimistic, and unforgettable few years of the Soviet cinema's glory will undoubtedly never be revived. Yet, traces of their art emerge in occasional flickers of genius that manage to cut through the ponderous prestige of an official cinema: an unending stream of "classic" adaptations of plays, operas, and ballets. Certainly, Kozintzev's Shakespearean films are worthy, often brilliant efforts, yet the sympathetic observer must admit that film as a contemporary art form in the USSR is presently impoverished, just as it has been for the last 25 years, by narrow formal and thematic conception.

In a cultural milieu where the artist is still closely scrutinized for signs of ideological unorthodoxy and strident individualism, it is remarkable that a filmmaker like Andrei Tarkovski has managed not only to survive but to create two of the most imposing Soviet films of the last decade. Following his bravura debut with *Ivan's Childhood*, he produced *Andrei Roublev*, a massive, but finely wrought, historical fresco depicting the personal struggles of the great icon painter, set against the painful turmoil of war and its attendant suffering that swept across feudal Russia.

Rather than create simply a biographic tribute, Tarkovski — in the tradition of Eisenstein — treats historic material as the vehicle for expressing his own beliefs and ideas, to develop the eternal and consequently always vital theme of the interrelation of an artist with his time, of the correlation between art and life. Tarkovski devoted three years to this epic work, which bears favorable comparison with the best of Eisenstein and Dovzhenko. Tarkovski himself defines the central subject as the individual suffering and sacrifice for the sake of an ideal: "The Russian people have always had a moral ideal, and Roublev endeavors to express it in his art. He succeeded in expressing this moral ideal of his epoch, the ideal of love, harmony, unity, and brotherhood."

Lofty sentiments were not sufficient, however, to endear the Russian critical front to this astonishing work as it mercilessly exposes the barbaric atmosphere of 15th century Russia with unprecedented realism, untempered by nobilized sentiments or events, though its concluding color images of the resplendent icons, suggest spiritual transcendence and rebirth. *Roublev* received limited showing in the Soviet Union, but was not distributed

Solaris

elsewhere for almost five years, though it registered a *succès d'estime* at Cannes in 1969 and appeared in selected European engagements the following year. (It ran for nearly a year at the Vieux-Colombier in Paris and was ecstatically received by the Paris press.)

Tarkovski's ranking in the vanguard of Soviet filmmakers and as an important creative force in modern cinema is confirmed by his most recent work, *Solaris,* a meditative parable based on the novel of the same title by the Polish science-fiction writer, Stanislas Lem, about the nature of scientific investigation and its limitations in coping with the irrational, and incomprehensible developments of cosmic exploration. Significantly, from a political as well as artistic perspective, he has moved from the historic past to a contemporary if somewhat theoretic subject and has again provoked considerable controversy, not only through the demanding stylistic nuance of the film, but also in its direct interrogation of the morality of science and man's position in the universe.

If the ambience is technically advanced and modern, *Solaris* — astutely referred to as a "Russian answer to *2001,*" is much less concerned with the aesthetics of technology than the emotional resonances of a scientific, technocratic society, which could be anywhere on earth, as the ambiguous character names and cultural setting indicate. At the same time, its thematic grandeur is classic, characteristic of the Russian novelistic imagination, preoccupied with central human existential dilemmas, the great themes of life, love, and death.

The opening prelude suggests a biological linkage between man and nature, a metaphor which gradually establishes itself as a connection between earth and the planet Solaris. A pond, with plantlife gently swaying, opens onto a quiet, poetic, lush country (Russian) landscape, where Chris Calvin, a middle-aged psychologist, contemplates the scene of his childhood prior to his impending journey to investigate a space station near the surface of Solaris.

In his father's country cottage, he confers with fellow cosmonauts, including Burton, who has returned from Solaris some years previously. They view a filmed report of Burton's interrogation by a scientific team, who in turn view films he has taken of the "visions" he experienced on the outpost. On earth scientists have hypothesized that the viscous surface of Solaris may actually be a living organism, but the science of Solaristics has run into a dead end for lack of definite, verifiable data, though Burton still insists that what he saw there was real.

Whereas Kubrick's *2001* follows with great fascination the journey of man and his streamlined apparatus on an interstellar mission, *Solaris* presents a metaphoric passage that, surprisingly, eliminates almost completely scenes of space travel. A futuristic

automotive transport is seen moving along an intersecting stretch of freeways and tunnels; the subjective, moving camera renders a flowing, musical sensation of movement through space, while the images, bathed in aqua tint, become increasingly darker, culminating in a full color shimmering superimposition of nocturnal traffic (astute observers have pointed out the locations as Tokyo). The interlude presents a marked contrast with the bucolic country scenes and its poetic analogue is made clear when Tarkovski cuts directly to a brief shot of distant stars as Chris approaches his destination and his space capsule descends to the orbital space station, hovering near the surface of Solaris. Here, for the first time, there is some of the awesome splendor of Kubrick's film, but only momentarily.

While the intricate, spacious decor of the space station is virtually expressionistic in design — each room and corridor suggesting a different psychological or emotional character — gadgets and machinery never overwhelm the human element nor are they endowed with anthropomorphisms. The atmosphere is at once ominous as Chris investigates the deserted, maze-like chambers and finally encounters only two remaining members of the original team of cosmic explorers: Dr. Snoutt, a scurrilous, short-tempered man, suffering from an unexplained source of psychic stress, who remains sealed off in his laboratory for long periods; and Sartorius, an older scientist whose resignation to loneliness and placid contemplation is unexpectedly interrupted by the visitor from earth who provokes in him a nervous apprehension.

Learning his comrade Gibaryan has recently committed suicide after a period of severe depression, Chris wanders dazed through his disordered living quarters to discover a filmed message — a communiqué from the dead — that does little to clarify the mystery surrounding the suicide and Sartorius is deliberately evasive in response to Chris' questioning. Thus Tarkovski, like many other modern directors evokes numerous narrative lines for which there are no given solutions.

Amid this labyrinthian observatory, a Cocteauesque "Zone" between life and death, in which unexplained phantoms flit through corridors and compartments, Chris soon learns that the sea of Solaris — the film's central metaphor — is a source of intel-

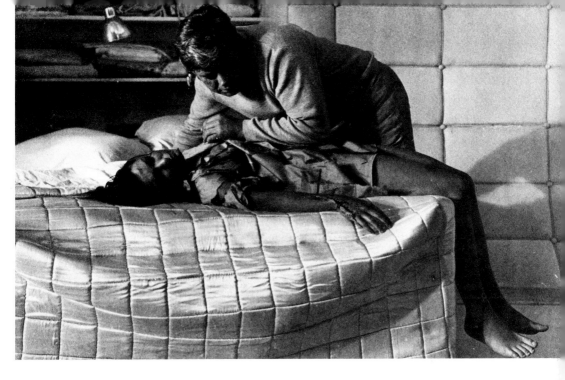

ligence, as suspected, and like the inexplicable monolith of *2001*, affects all within its immediate proximity. Images and visions, referred to as "visitors" — actually materializations derived from the human brain — appear periodically to haunt the men. Chris remains somewhat skeptical until he begins to experience the reincarnation of Hari, his beautiful young wife who ended her own life on earth, many years previously.

The revival of Chris' love for Hari, an emotion relegated to the museum of memory, is central to Tarkovski's thematic structure. The apparition of Hari, beautifully captured in dream images, moving from aqua tints as Chris prepares for sleep, to golden, transcendent light, evokes profound feelings in Chris. As Hari becomes more and more human, prompted by Chris' attempt to stir memories of her earthly existence, he becomes increasingly distressed by his failure and the knowledge — evidenced by Snoutt — that she is in fact, biologically, "inhuman." Chris plummets her into space in a rocket, but she reappears and twice recovers from fatal accidents; and when he ultimately surrenders to her growing love, she realizes the mental anguish it is causing and departs never to return.

The suffering brought on by this experience forces Chris to understand a universal truth: that the most vital things in life, whatever form it may assume, cannot always be verified; the cosmos is a vast reflection of the mystery of love, a phenomenon man can experience but never perfectly understand, and before which science is helpless. Experience equally directs Chris to the sea of Solaris, the enigmatic source of this mental suffering. Sartorius, the film's spokesman for scientific conservatism and tradition, proposes that risk must be minimized if their work is to continue, by

beaming lethal rays at the ocean, and sees no validity in Chris' emotional attachment to his "visitor." Chris however, asserts that science must always be guided by moral principles and that to destroy any living matter simply because man cannot understand it is unethical. In a meditative soliloquy before the sentient surface of the planet, he professes that the ocean is seeking to penetrate the ideas of man and that they must respond by providing it with precise data about mankind in an orderly way, rather than through fragments of dreams.

An encephelographic record of Chris' private thoughts is projected onto the sea of Solaris, calming its turbulence, and suddenly islands begin to surface. With awesome effect, the film's final sequence, a formal variation on the opening prelude, returns to the pond and country landscape; but as Chris observes them, natural processes are reduced to stasis, with only the movement of the man and a dog against the frozen background. But as the camera pulls back to encompass the house where Chris warmly greets his father, then moves further and further back into space, we gradually see this is a materialization on an island in the sea of Solaris. . . .

The spiritual complexity of the vision Tarkovski has derived from Lem's novel organically unites man with the mysteries of the cosmos, and finds expression in a style that is essentially metaphysical and poetic. The visual continuity is synthetic and organic, emphasizing sustained *mise-en-scène* rather than an analytical shot breakdown, and the use of Panavision ratio is perfectly suited to the stylistic mode. Inevitably, Tarkovski will be criticized for the solemn, slow pacing of the film, though it is quite intentional. Just as Kubrick indicates our experience of time will be radically affected by space travel, Tarkovski retards the movement of the individual shot, the camera and actors, to render a temporal duration that is an aesthetic equivalent totally removed from our present hectic psycho-perceptual experience. Occasionally there is a sense of *temps-morts* in Chris' prolonged preparation for sleep, fleeting memories of earth, and the haunting moments dwelling on the viscous surface of Solaris.

The film's mesmeric, poetic rhythm requires an unaccustomed patience and attention, considering its exceptional length of two and three-quarter hours, but it is arguably an integral and essential part of the director's expression. Music is sparingly but effectively used with the plaintive organ tones of Bach's F Minor Choral Prelude underscoring scenes suggesting ties between earth and outer space, supplemented by amplified percussion, an appropriate "music of the spheres."

Tarkovski's intimate acting ensemble, all experienced in theatre as well as cinema, are superbly attuned to the sustained level of dramatic understatement and introspection. Without possessing any of the physical appeal of a major film star, Donatas Banionis, a Georgian actor, is authoritative and persuasive in the central role of Chris Calvin, while his more impressive interlocuter Sartorius, is memorably etched by the cragged nobility of Yuri Jarvet, who gave life to Kozintzev's King Lear. In the brief but pungent role of Dr. Snoutt is Anatoly Solonitsyn, the lead in Tarkovski's *Andrei Roublev*; Natalie Bondarchuk, daughter of the actor/director Sergei Bondarchuk not only is strikingly beautiful but projects a tender, ethereal presence as Hari, and her enactment of revivification after a suicide attempt by drinking liquid oxygen is extraordinarily vivid.

With an art that tends to conceal its virtuosity, Tarkovski, with his co-scenarist F. Gorenchstein and cameraman Vadim Youssov, has invested every detail of the film with the care of a Tolstoi or Cervantes. *Solaris* is at once personal and universal, timeless, and yet the most imaginative subject in modern Soviet cinema. It is a major work in the as yet slender and provocative body of Tarkovski's *oeuvre*, and is a testament to his creative daring that refuses to be silenced.

Fahrenheit 451

SELECTIVE BIBLIOGRAPHY

Books

Agel, Jerome, ed. *The Making of Kubrick's 2001*. New York: Signet Film Series, 1970.

Amis, Kingsley. *New Maps of Hell*. New York: Harcourt Brace Jovanovich, 1960.

Baxter, John. *Science Fiction in the Cinema*. New York: A. S. Barnes, 1969.

Clarens, Carlos. *An Illustrated History of the Horror Film*. New York: Putnam, 1968.

Eisner, Lotte H. *The Haunted Screen*. Berkeley and Los Angeles: University of California, 1969.

Geduld, Carolyn. *Filmguide to 2001: A Space Odyssey*. Bloomington: Indiana University Press, 1973.

Gifford, Denis. *Movie Monsters*. New York: Dutton, 1969.

_____. *Science Fiction Film*. New York: Dutton, 1971.

Hammond, Paul. *Marvelous Méliès*. New York: St. Martin's Press, 1975.

Harryhausen, Ray. *Film Fantasy Scrapbook*, second edition, revised. South Brunswick and New York: A. S. Barnes, 1974.

Hutchinson, Toni. *Horror and Fantasy in the Movies*. New York: Crown, 1974.

Jensen, Paul M. *The Cinema of Fritz Lang*. New York: A. S. Barnes, 1969.

Johnson, William, ed. *Focus on the Science Fiction Film*. New Jersey: Prentice-Hall, 1972.

Kaminsky, Stuart M. *American Film Genres: Approaches to a Critical Theory of Popular Film*. Dayton: Pflaum Publishing, 1974.

Lee, Walter W., Jr. *Reference Guide to Fantastic Films*, Vols. 1-3. Los Angeles: Chelsea-Lee, 1972-74.

Sadoul, Georges. *Georges Méliès*. Paris: Seghers, 1961.

Science Fiction Films from 1895 to 1930. London: British Film Institute, 1966.

Steinbrunner, Chris and Burt Goldblatt. *Cinema of the Fantastic*. New York: Saturday Review Press, 1972.

Whitfield, Stephen E., and Gene Roddenberry. *The Making of Star Trek*. New York: Ballantine, 1968.

Magazine Articles

Atkins, Thomas R. "The Illustrated Man: An Interview with Ray Bradbury," *Sight and Sound*, 43, 2 (Spring 1974).

Colloquy, IV, 5 (May 1971). Special issue on science fiction.

Geduld, Harry M. "Return to Méliès: Reflections on the Science Fiction Film," *The Humanist*, 28, 6 (November/December 1968).

Houston, Penelope. "Glimpses of the Moon." *Sight and Sound*, 22, 3 (April-June 1953).

Landrum, Larry N. "A Checklist of Materials about Science Fiction Films of the 1950's," *Journal of Popular Film*, I, 1 (Winter, 1972).

Lightman, Herb A. "Filming *2001: A Space Odyssey*," *American Cinematographer*, 49 (June 1968).

Midi/Minuit Fantastique, 3 (1962). Special issue on *King Kong* and *The Lost World*.

Murphy, Brian. "Monster Movies: They Came From Beneath the Fifties," *Journal of Popular Film*, I, 1 (Winter 1972).

Schwartz, Nancy. "*THX 1138* vs. *Metropolis*: The New Politics of Science Fiction Film," *The Velvet Light Trap*, 4 (Spring 1972).

Sontag, Susan. "The Imagination of Disaster," *Against Interpretation*. New York: Farrar, Straus & Giroux, 1965.

Tarratt, Margaret. "Monsters From the Id," *Films and Filming* (December 1970 and January 1971).

Wharton, Lawrence. "*Godzilla* to *Latitude Zero:* The Cycle of the Technological Monster," *Journal of Popular Film*, III, 1 (Winter 1974).

Magazines
(either devoted to science fiction films or containing sf material)

Castle of Frankenstein. Gothic Castle Publishing Co., Inc., 509 Fifth Avenue, New York, N.Y. 10017.

Cinefantastique. P.O. Box 270, Oak Park, Illinois 60635.

Famous Monsters of Filmland. Warren Publishing Co., 145 East 32nd Street, New York, N.Y. 10016.

Photon. 801 Avenue "C", Brooklyn, N.Y. 11218.

The Journal of Popular Film. University Hall 101, Bowling Green University, Bowling Green, Ohio 43403.

The Incredible Shrinking Man

1976

C